S0-ALE-198

WOOD

ACKNOWLEDGEMENTS

Thank you to...

My thoughtful and tireless editor, Brian Kaufman, and everyone at Anvil Press.

The editors of the following publications, who first published some of the poems in this book: *subTerrain, Event, PRISM International, Misfit Lit, Ripe, Numero Cinq, The Fiddlehead*.

Judy and Ben Harper, and everyone in my family.

The thoughtful and loving first readers of these poems: Marita Dachsel, Laisha Rosnau, Colin Campbell.

Jeff Morris, for the title *Wood*, and so much more.

Wood

POEMS

by

JENNICA HARPER

ANVIL PRESS | 2013

Copyright © 2013 by Jennica Harper

First edition: September 2013

All rights reserved. No part of this publication may be reproduced or transmitted in any form or by any means, electronic or mechanical, including photocopying, recording or by any information storage and retrieval system now known or to be invented, without permission in writing from the publisher.

Anvil Press gratefully acknowledges the support of the Government of Canada through the Canada Book Fund, the Canada Council for the Arts, and the Province of British Columbia through the British Columbia Arts Council.

NATIONAL LIBRARY OF CANADA CATALOGUING IN PUBLICATION DATA

Harper, Jennica, 1975-, author
        Wood / Jennica Harper.

ISBN 978-1-927380-64-2 (pbk.)

        I. Title.

PS8565.A6421W66 2013   C811'.6   C2013-904802-2

Cover design by Rayola Graphic
Interior design by HeimatHouse
Author photo by Pardeep Singh

Anvil Press Publishers
P.O. Box 3008, Main Post Office
Vancouver, B.C. Canada
V6B 3X5
www.anvilpress.com

Printed and bound in Canada.

CONTENTS

7

REALBOYS

23

LINER NOTES

37

PAPA HOTEL

45

THE BOX

63

WOULD

79

ROOTS: THE SALLY DRAPER POEMS

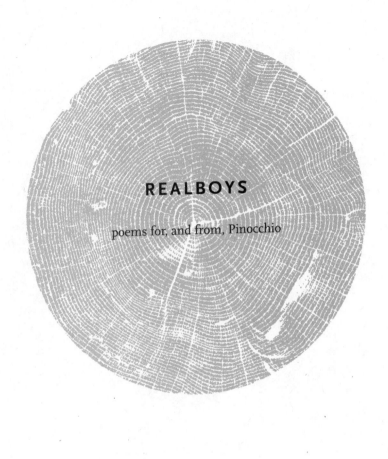

REALBOYS

poems for, and from, Pinocchio

REALBOYS & THE CRICKET

Father told me realboys have something inside
them that tells them what is right and wrong, clever
or foolish. This Mindcricket is completely silent,
heard only by the realboy inside his skullbone. It can
spring up at any time, warning of poor decisions
about to be made, such as burying goldpieces and
waiting for them to bloom. I'm no longer sure I want
to be a realboy. I can squish my Cricket with a broom.

EDUCATION

Cindy A. sits in front of me. I'm learning to sit still, say
nothing. By saying nothing, nothing good nor bad
can happen. Good odds for bad boys like me. But
Cindy A... Cindy A., when she puts up her hand,
her back spoons like an oar. I think of Ms. Blue, her
blue dress   shoulderbones   blue dust   her collarbone.
I think of two oars, sculling. Then I think of nothing.

There is a knock on wood. Glances to the door, standing
open — no one's there. Eyes turn my way. I shut mine
tight, avoiding Cindy A's. In my lap, wood meets wood.
The friction feels good...all through spelling, I buff
I whet, until I worry my worrying will spark a blaze.
Fear of fire makes me good again at last. It hurts
to stop, but I do. After school I hold my spellingbook
in front of me as though very proud to be a pupil.

BECOMING A MAN

Father hopes I will become a realboy because
realboys become men. Good men take over
the family business or learn a new trade,
bringing in goldpieces for their families.
Money's good. Money's traded for food,
money keeps the rain out. I've tried to carve
wood, Father showed me the *shwick!*
of the knife, but I'm scared of the knife,
and to me the wood looked fine as it was.

CRICKET

on Duty

So I take a few breaks, no one's on the clock alla time.
Ain't exactly a bargain for me either, okay.

The kid don't learn. Does the same stupid shit, again and again,
always surprised it gets fucked and he gets caught.

I once watched the same pussy pull the *same con* on the kid
two nights in a row. Show him a few coins, he loses
the piss-little-bit a sense he got.

It ain't so much his fault. Kid got no...heart. Soul. Whatever.

Boy ain't bad.
He just ain't a person.

PLANS

Last night Father told me he wishes to be burned to ash.
To take up as little space as possible, then ride on wind
currents, racing dandelion seeds, seeing the world.

I dreamt of the box burning up around me. I wouldn't catch.

MS. BLUE
on Growing

Sweet child wants so badly
to be a man. How hard it was
to tell him he'll always be
a sapling. Puppets
don't grow.

I tried to explain —

Being a man
is more than
height, shoulders,
voice deepening to
baritone. We talked
about courage,
confidence.

Grace.

He wept, and, blinded by
his tears, the poor dear
reached out and
touched my breast.

TRANSFORMATION

I was almost a donkey. It would be easier.
I could pull carts full of wares and be useful,
and not think about not being a donkey. I would
sleep, and I bet I would not dream, and if I
dreamed they would be a donkey's dreams. But
knowing me, I would ruin it. Dream of nothing
but having my shabby coat brushed by a girl.

WORK

i.

I have a job! I have something to fill my days and keep me from
an idlemind. As Father begins his day in his workshop, I put on
my uniform and go. I'm good at my work. Better than the others.
I pretend to watch the screen, with its flat shapes and bright lines,
looking for odd clusters of wires. Actually I watch the people. How
they dump change from their pockets, take off their shoes. All
the clues I need. I can tell from a slump or blink or liplick, who
is trying to hide from me. No one has my nose, but a lie still shows.
I guess it takes one to know one.

ii.

I love work but wish they would not give me money. There are
too many places to spend it on the way home. Open doors,
with stairs that lead up. They know my name. Pull my strings.
Father, can you understand? In carving me, you made me
rigid with the need to be made over and over. Whittled down
to nothing, then, with gentle hands, oil in the grain, reshaped
into the me I show to you.

PROMISES

Father talks little of the God. But I understand.
The God is the one who made Father out of notwood.
When Father promises to be good, it's to the God.

I have not seen the Cricket in weeks. He has given up —
moved on to some other maybe-realboy, some unburled
heartwood. I know why. I break things, yet nothing
breaks me. I make things hard.

WHERE IT GOES

Gepetto dies.
But it is taking some time.

All year he has grown smaller. Skin
hanging, where he once was fuller.
I do not know where he disappears to.

The thing that is real: is it in his blood,
travelling through him still? The parts that
are gone now: were they not real?

Father goes from bed to toilet, toilet to sink.
He won't look me in the eye.

I have done this to him. He tried to make
me more, and has made himself less.
Given up parts of himself.
Parts he needs.

I would give him mine —

But I have no blood to offer. No cells,
no jellyseeds racing through
veins I do not have.

I have no organmeat to spare you, Father.

Father whispers. Tells me
this is all as it should be. This is real.
What we both wanted.

His whisper, paper.

I know he is trying to tell me something
I do not understand. He says a son
and his father are always wishing to trade.

In arithmetic, each number exists.
In algebra, numbers are letters.

A letter stands in for a number.
It seems it could be any number...
but it is a particular one.

Particular, but only in agreement
with other particular numbers.
It is all or nothing.

But why can you not add A to B?

I always said "father." Only now
does Father say "son." I do not cry.

I say:
I would stand in for you, Father.

Even before I feel the familiar throb,
I know it is a lie.

EVERY GOOD BOY

Every good boy deserves fun. Every good boy deserves food. Every good boy deserves a father. Every good boy deserves forgiveness. Boy, everybody's good. How did they get so good? Father says I'm good wood — when he's in a good mood. Good wood deserves food, fun, fudge, favours, fairy dust. Every good boy deserves dessert. Everyboy wants. Even good ones would. God wood. Even good boys desert fathers. Fairyblood, realbody, borrowed air, floatboy. Whoa. Am I being rood? Every good block of wood...I *know* I know it, give me a minute.

LINER NOTES

Limbs unthinking,
she's on the living room floor.
The TV on behind her.
Her eyes loll, unfocused, lost
to their discrete orbits,

but open wide.
Like they're taking their time,
trying to decide.

She's beautiful. No question.
Her chocolate hair fans around her face
as she lies there, waiting.

That toothy smile she's quick to share.

Can beauty
be wasted?

I want a taste; want to know
what it means to be beautiful,
to know nothing of it.

*

Remote: I turn off the TV.
She knows it's me,
knows who I am by smell,
blur of colour, how
I move —

I betray myself
with every molecule.

I don't know any person
as instinctively
as she knows me.

I come here
twice a week.

It's my job to stimulate. To prevent boredom, laziness,
pointlessness, fruitlessness, bedsores —

to, for three hours,
let her mother and father
think about not her.

*

She's wondering what we'll do today:
will I put her hands in clay or paint?

    Paint is great. She loves the feel
    of wet hands. Loves to squish.

    My hands on her hands.
    My hands are her hands.

    I remember how good it feels
    to squish.

But paint is also
messy.

Not today.

*

She's three, and really not so different
from other three-year-olds. She can barely see,
hear, sit up. Has no language. But she looks happy.

It won't be sad until she's ten.

When she's twenty, a problem for health care.

*

I crank the stereo. Tommy James sings
"Crimson and Clover" —
my favourite, from the family's
small collection.

The worst: anything by the Beach Boys.
"Good Vibrations" is so on the nose.
An anthem for the deaf.

Others I won't play:
"I Can See Clearly Now"
"Pinball Wizard"
"Don't Worry, Be Happy."

I place my hands over her hands.

We pat together, a half beat behind, or ahead.

Her mother and father argue
in the kitchen like dishwashers
going through their cycles.

They shout the shouts
of the very tired.

*

We're patting,
patting.

Now I don't hardly know her…
But I think I could love her…

I put the song on a loop.
Let her just lie there, feel it, while

I flip through Tommy's
liner notes.

*

In 1969, Tommy James & the Shondells turned down an offer to perform at Woodstock when their booking agent described the event as "…a stupid gig on a pig farm in upstate New York."

I am going to New York City in two weeks,
to see my boyfriend
of ten months.

We will see if I come back
with a broken heart
or just single.

I want to see a Broadway show,
and Central Park.

I 💔 NY.

*

Ten months together feels like years.
In the beginning, the danger of it:

      fumbling under blankets
      in his parents' basement

      in doorways, in taxis, the pleasure,
      desire wanting an answer

      always
      having its way

Lately, in bland afternoon light,
we barely look at one another.

*

Her eyes search for me.

She is wondering what is coming.

Will I put her feet
in those awful braces —

make her stand up, feet grounded
in hard moon-boots, hands in my hands —

her rigid body swaying like birch?

I might.

*

"Mony Mony" is still frequently played at weddings
where guests yell profane responses between the lines.

I know I will not marry my boyfriend.
Husband, wife, father, mother, oh brother —
the summer drags on.

Ten months,

                    wasted.

Tommy James & the Shondells went on vacation in 1969
and never got back together.

The gentlest of breakups —
a happy separation, and then —

just never finding your way together again.

*

My mind's such a sweet thing...

We are alone, she and I, two bodies
in a room, both blips on a forgotten radar.

We are two hearts, two brains, two UFOS
crash-landed on a brown carpet.

The world forgets us for a while, and we don't mind.

*

The arguing in the kitchen gets louder.
How can we possibly —
Oh, grow up!

I wrap her up in a puffy pink jacket,
sit her in a stroller meant
for someone younger,

a child not finished yet.

This is no place for
young girls like us.

*

A kite tied to the handle of her stroller
lolls like a useless tongue;
I pick it up and carry it.

We need to find some sun,
sky, grass, happy people.

What a beautiful feeling...

*

Babies have five senses like everyone else.
But they don't have the ability to seek out stimulus.
It has to be brought to them.

I pick a dandelion —
she won't know the difference
between flower and weed —
hold it under her nose.

She doesn't know what to do.

She is not
a baby.

But today, she is mine.

*

Ten months is a long time
in the life of a child. Or a hit single.

US listeners got sick of "Crimson and Clover" quickly. It went from #1 to #18
to completely off the charts in two weeks, setting a record

for furthest,
fastest fall.

*

What is the difference between a flower and a weed?

Not beauty.

Weeds are parasitic, sometimes poisonous, hosts for pests.
Wild, feral.

Trouble.

*

There are various interpretations of the meaning of "Crimson and Clover"
ranging from innocent (the colours of a high school crush's plaid skirt)
to theological (the blood of Christ, the clover's holy trinity) to vulgar
(sex during menstruation, the "clover" slang for female genitalia) to brutal
(the slaughtering of a girl in a field).

Many continue to believe it's simply about being high, floating, synesthesia,
letting go.

*

I walk the stroller under the viaduct,
the only way to the park.

Cars thunder above. Like the end of the world.

She bangs her fist to her forehead,
pounds, pounds,
searching for the beat —

I take her hand in mine,
press hard —
tell her *no*.

When she stops hitting herself,
we leave the shadows of the tunnel
and the sun's heat hits her.

She blinks.

The world
is born again.

*

Soon it will be fall, so
fast. Beginning of second year.

I don't know who I'll marry,
and at this moment?
I'm not sure I care.

*

In the park, kids on tire swings. A game of tag.
I'm happy she doesn't know what she's missing.

The rhythm of the playground is in relief —

feels deliberate —

a song unheard —

waste, waste, waste, waste, waste —

*

In the middle of "Crimson and Clover," the pace picks up.
Mimics — what? A heart racing —
fear
anger
lust —
something you see coming.

Something you look right
in the eyes.

*

— the kite tugs itself out of my hand, and lifts.
Pulls its own weight up
away from the earth —
sways, a UFO in primaries —

she is looking right at it and laughing.

PAPA HOTEL

MY FATHER, AS JACK NICHOLSON

A man who knows a pretty girl when he sees one, and he's always seeing one. He reads waitresses' tags, calls them their names. All down-home Daddy drawl. When he was young, this probably worked with some. Now they humour him. For some reason I want them to be spellbound, charmed, hot, as they listen to what he does and does not want.

AS ROBERT REDFORD

Not the brilliant reporter, the baseball player. The underdog who did it his own way, who made that bat out of his Own Goddamn Wood, and won. This man is the golden boy. Parade-worthy. But after, nothing feels real. He'll have indigestion, insomnia. He'll stare at the bat, having no memory of making it. Get up in the middle of the night and just drive, not knowing what made him go. This man will take in his hand a whole clump of tinsel and throw it at the Christmas tree. Letting it go where it wants, letting it land where it lands.

AS KEVIN COSTNER

Redford's evil baseball-playing twin. The one who sweats too much
and likes to fuck, and keeps on fucking until his children are old enough
to understand and then still keeps on, perhaps more so. The man who
sings both *Mama, don't let your babies grow up to be cowboys* and *Thank God
I'm a country boy.* This man is not a team player. He's the rule-breaker
who eventually loses it all, who can't take the heat so he burns down
the kitchen. The man who's made up of a billion tiny anger cells erupting
constantly — the man who gave me those chains, those loops and
numbers that flare in me, red and white and hot, when I think of him.

AS ROMAN POLANSKI

Not welcome. A trail of broken wives and dead babies in his past, he wanders
obscurely through brown streets in Paraguay, buying only the cheapest items
for his family at home: thin linens, turquoise beads like painted rabbit turds.
We receive the gifts like anyone receives any gift: hopefully, anxiously. That night
the linens are folded at the end of my bed, too close to the gerbil's cage, and she
eats holes in them. It's my dream-persona tearing at the stringy white blouse
and skirt, I eat until they're good and ruined and then I wake. In the morning,
Mom finds me crying and tells me they're only things, and hurt things never
deserve to be cried over the way you'd cry over a hurt person. When he sees
the holey shrouds, his face goes cold. He tells me how much he paid.

AS PETER FALK

All nervous looks and words. All style. Not a trenchcoat, but dirty jeans
and a gray sweater, patched elbows. Not a cigar: a carved pipe like a lion's
head. No questions — he's more about those silences, when I think he knows
something but isn't saying. Detectives keep strange hours, are often gone
in the middle of the night. All the next day too. One time he finds me,
the sleepwalker, bent on the stairs. I don't know when or how I got there, only
that I expected him to be home earlier in my dreams. He lifts me up, carries
me back to my bleached-wood captain's bed. Tells me not to tell Mom how late
it was, best not to worry her. The pillow sinks under the weight of my face, and
I tell him not to worry, I won't remember in the morning.

AS STEVE MCQUEEN

He's riding in a convertible, wind tossing his fluffy hair straight up
and around, snaking the streets of San Fran, looking for someone to
outshine. He looks like a boy. My son will look like this: white-blond hair,
freckle-smeared skin. Will be better off in the shade but will be drawn to open
sheets of sunlit grass. He'll ignore the warnings, will try to live speeding,
remain airborne.

My father pulls back gently on a lever in a helicopter, and eases us into wide
airspace. I am co-pilot for the first time; I am seven. The barcode crops extend
beneath us, and fill up the margins. Then we hover near encroaching cliff faces
on the way to Lake Temagami, where Dad has some work to do. He speaks
into his walkie-talkie, says numbers and code words, Victor and Hotel,
Papa and Oscar. For a moment I understand this, his native language, and
want to speak it too.

From a distance, we must look like a mechanical fly, buzzing stupidly along
the edges of badland cliff walls, looking for some way out, some window. But
inside it feels nice, the air is thick and warm, and there's only enough room
for the two of us.

THE BOX

Erik Weisz (Harry Houdini)
married Wilhelmina Beatrice Rahner (Bess)
on June 22, 1894.

They had no children.

CONEY ISLAND HONEYMOON

i.

Now I'm the wife of the Handcuff King. Royalty
of New York. The man who can escape anything
but awkwardness. You, who is always the shortest

man in the room, but still you draw eyes like
some trick with magnets. All of us filings on your smooth
plane. But there are limits, even for you.

You can only outdo yourself so many times
before it's just aesthetic: the woman sawn in half
with a scimitar this time.
                              It is cold

on our Coney Island Honeymoon. The lights are low,
everything is a geometric puzzle: the Ferris wheel
and carousel churn their mechanical roundelay,

and somewhere the funambulist plucks his taut wire.
Everything is simple lines but you and I are round,
compact, soft, easily broken down limb by limb:

this is the arm I pull through first, this is the wrist I bend backward.
This is the foot I twist. These are the lips I will kiss you with.
Am I cold? We are dressed for a day, but not this one.

ii.

After the kiss, I know you're watching the machines,
plotting how to make them dumb and dull. I want
something to stay hidden. You, in too much clothing,

your pant cuffs crumpled like elephant feet. An idea
of a man in there somewhere, an ordinary man, waiting to pop out
with a *sproing!* and *ta-da*, but everything is obscured by the damn fog.

And a part of me wants it like this.
Never to understand, only to cling to your back,
a wrinkle you will not smooth away.

My mind goes back and back to the kiss:
I can feel the echo of a stitch, a dozen needles swallowed,
then threaded, one by one by one,

and coming back up in a long line,
striating my throat, diamonds on the clothesline,
new constellation on a wire.

SOMETIMES

Sometimes his kiss is quick,

a skipped-over word, as if understood.
A blink.
As though neither of us is in the room
but our lips cross paths in time.

*

Sometimes it is slow and salty:
too ripe wine —

                    a hand covering an eye.

*

But that sounds too simple.
          Most times
it comes out of nowhere,   my own
kiss catching up   but barely,
heart fissuring,

both hands over eyes
but fingers parted:

sun and cloud and sun and cloud.

DREAM CHILD #1

Greta is a good girl, enjoys her schooling
and defends those weaker than herself.

She was born on a Sunday, and knows the rhyme
(blithe, bonny, good, gay) by heart.

When she was eight, she stood on the corner
downtown, shouted to anyone passing

that kindness takes you further than its twin.
That those who invited others into their homes

and hearts would go to Heaven. And those
who were cold and kept to themselves

would be alone forever. Sweet Greta,
who believes in yes's and no's,

does not see spaces in between.
I fear she will have a tough time of it.

TRICKS

1. Walking Through a Wall

This one requires a diagram
to understand: a rug is laid on the floor
of the stage. A brick wall — authentic,
and examined by a member
of the audience! — is set upon it.
A screen is placed on either
side of the wall; you slip behind
one screen and lo, emerge
from the screen on the other side,
miraculous. Whole.
(There is a trapdoor beneath.
The rug sags just enough
to allow you to slither under.)
Do they not guess at
the truth? The rug?
For goodness sake, the screens?

2. Sawing a Woman in Half

Everyone knows how this one's done.
The trick's not in mistaking it for real.
The trick is how it makes one feel:
the gut-knot longing to come undone.

A man watches and wonders if, just this time,
something will go wrong and there'll be blood.
A screech, she's split, tries to claw from the wood —
A woman watches and hopes the same.

3. The Box

Under our covers
I think of the rug sagging
The sawn woman, buckling

My heart is a wet vegetable
Sitting in its cold box
It may be malformed, useless,
Rotten

What a trick
That you've not wondered

DREAM CHILD #2

Lucy is afraid of sunlight,
open spaces.

When she was one week old, her cries
sucking, dying sounds in the dark,

I held her in the L of my arm,
purred into her ear. Hushed

spells of love and protection,
called her my one, my bug —

my precious doll. She wouldn't stop
so I put her in the trunk, covered her face

with a blanket, closed the Steamer's top.
She slept like a clenched fist 'til morning.

RESTRAINT

Last night we dirtied all the bowls in the house, filled them with nuts, grapes, creams. Ate half of everything, then went to bed as a draft in the hall slammed a door silly.

The gramophone collects dust. When we read we read in different rooms.

Next to me, you fought with your pillow. I could only make out the blur of you and the red of the pillowcase. Your arm an arc of aggression, a thing to be tamed, or taunted into play.

Our life: plywood trickery, empty spaces. Secrets put down on paper and locked away.

Your feet were so cold, I wanted to turn the fan off and sing for you like I used to. Be your chickadee, your voice.

Dull things prettied up by velvet.

But you rolled over, dove into sleep in the hope you would come up heaving, different, lungs aching but awake. I closed my eyes.

A straitjacket in the hamper. Long arms like a mother, arms long enough to wrap around me twice.

SHADOWBOXING

You know there is nothing magical
in sex with an escape artist.

Either he is full of tricks, all
pomp and sound…

…or he is there, hot breath
in your ear, while you wait.

*

You'd prefer Sherlock Holmes
to Doyle. You believe the detective to be
a magnificent lover: ridged fingertips
reeking of tobacco, cheeks
like long blank pages.

And a singular focus. Clarity
with the task at hand.

Yet Doyle is the one with five children
(on the books). Though he tries to
put down his quill — to quit
spilling, to kill
Holmes — you know he never will.

*

The man you might have
married: a long man in a long
wool coat. No sense of humour.
The thought of him makes you warm,
makes you shudder.

*

Her husband's torso: a clay bowl,
neatly shaped with loving hands
but fired with pockets of air.
Only a matter of time.

His wife's bowl: grainy, ringed,
open hands,
hoping to carry.

*

You envy Bess,
a dead woman.

She knows how
it all turned out.

*

You want a bowl
of your own,
NO —

a *blow* of your own.
You long to be hit in the jaw
or nose, no time to cry out.
You feel the bomb of fist,
a moment later, the white flash.
You want someone
to not hold back, you want
to be bruised
from the outside.

*

You want her to leave him
because you won't.

THE UPSIDE-DOWN

For once, we sit in the crowd, the children
allowed to watch their father, the performer.
We've decided they're old enough to see
you hang upside-down, fight for breath.
The Chinese Water Torture Cell! Torture
sells, no doubt about that. Your ankles
in stocks, you're dipped down, the water
rising all around you. But your eyes
are clear, focused on the little ones so
they know you are going to be all right.
The curtain closes. I feel Greta stop breathing,
nudge her side so she'll start again. Remember
what I said, sweetheart. It's a show. *I know.*
When the curtains part, you're wet
but out, and again, your eyes go right to them,
so they know contact was never really
broken. They love it, want to come back
tomorrow, and my heart sinks as I realize
why. Here, you looked at their faces, were
tethered to them, rather than rushing by.

With a start, I look down at the little ones,
see only the anesthetized faces of strangers.

LAST TRICK

Nothing makes sense:
you tell me about the punch,
the fist in your soft, unreadied
gut. But, after all, it was just one blow

you're still not an old man
and this won't be the last time
you'll fall into bed cringing,
unable to take off your clothes.

You don't want to talk about the kid,
and I can read your face: you are
straining to speak at all,
your heart racing — mine too

but instead of saying anything,
you reach up, take my hand,
pull me down onto the bed.
Finger my buttons.

I am winged, and you are the king
      of diamonds, your hair all red waves
           You're a cliff face, and I'm plunging off, into
               the ocean, my skirts puffed up with air

      flying,
    billowing,
  a bellows
    filling

(but it's not me filling up —

not my gut)

Then, a winded groan
as I go under.

WIFE

Her imagined children are your imagined children. For all you know she was content, childless, her small womb unstretched, a balloon never blown. Her belly skin taut 'til the end. You want her to want those children. Then she'd be missing something, like you. You know it may have been enough for her: trailing after a husband, compact like a gymnast but head the size of Kalamazoo. It may have been enough for you, too. But you doubt it. How long before the novelty of hotel rooms wears off, gets dull, like silver left too long unpolished in a drawer? Surely toward the end she felt like a balloon blown too full, floating in the sky, not a soul in sight. No child to grab her, promise to not let go, hang on tight. Instead, hovering on the sidelines, waiting for her famous husband to need her, standing around, key in her mouth.

DREAM CHILD #3

Teddy rocks himself
in the rocking chair,
falls asleep there, small peach-head
resting on the arm,
a statue — though I don't recall
ever seeing a statue
of a child. He wakes only
when the chair is still.

When he is older,
he'll rock himself to sleep
in bed, rolling gently
back and forth,
hips swivelling
like they're impatient
for a dance.

I'm sure the dreams of children
are different: more like their
waking lives. Nothing hoped-for
perched on a trapdoor.

I remember the ferry to Staten Island,
head bent overboard,
tossing up dinner, a feast
for the fishes. But you, little egg,
must have loved the waves
rolling back upon themselves
like patient second thoughts.

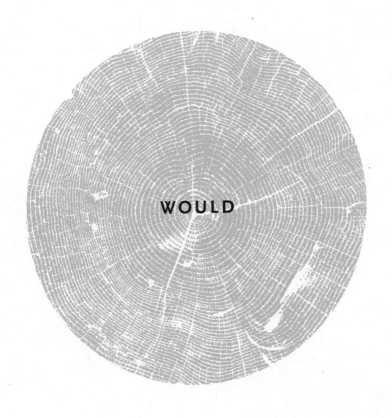

WOULD

FOR THE BORDENS,
UNABLE TO HAVE CHILDREN

A terrible Tuesday: Andrew and Abby struck down
by food poisoning. Cheap mutton left out too long.
Man and wife sleep in separate rooms, shiver
in their own worlds, so as not to stare into a shared
slop bucket. The maid, Bridget, suffers in a room upstairs —
her prayers for sleep interrupted by sick. It seems
the end has come. And yet,

Wednesday arrives. And an appetite.
Andrew rises, calls to Bridget to put on a meal.
Goes to his wife's room, where the morning sun
slices through, splitting Abby's face
in light and gentle shadow. Her fever has broken
too. Andrew does not know how many years
of this — being pried apart, drifting back together
— they will have. But it is enough. Before he leans
to kiss her cheek, her eyes open. She is back.

FEVER

When he's gone she clicks the link, submits
her criteria through drop-down menus:
2 or more bedrooms under 500 K.
She waits for red dots to appear, a pox
she hopes to catch. No unique questions here:
do we want a lawn to mow? We would need a lawnmower.
Do we want a Korean girl in the lower, practicing her
violin? No matter: no hits. At best it's three quarters of a mil
for a teardown. Or an East-side special, kid sister with a lisp.
Still, there's hope in the glow…she rejigs, refines
her search, such fun at first, she knows she should stop when
the rub turns raw. The grass always greener in Dunbar.
But maybe. Maybe today there's a high enough ceiling.
Once more, knock wood for the happy ending.

CLOUD SISTERS

1. Growth Capacity

Some days we look the same,
depending on our hair:

blunt cut under the ears.
Dirty blonde, the dye gone.

We are older now. Have
filled our skins.

Have filled our lives with
others' lives, and living.

2. Metabolism

Life's a process that goes
on without you noticing.

Thank our chemicals. Why
I call or do not call

always comes down to energy.
If I were better I would save

up more for you. I burn it
not even knowing where it goes.

3. Reproduction

Have you noticed it's not
just us in the room now?

The pink-cheeked child
is yours but could be mine.

Our parents are siblings
and are so unalike. They

seem like strangers.
What are we?

4. Adaptation to Environment

We are cloud sisters.
We pass, move, blow, cover.

The anaphase surprised us,
but we're recovering well.

I think about you even when
I don't call. The sky's batting

keeps us together, full of
each other: woven; the same.

THE LOSS

You imagined — and you did imagine — a quiet loss.
A tender evening, some tears, some talk, then move on.

Instead, the E.R. when the bleeding won't stop. Panic
when you can't eat the bagel you bought; in case you need

surgery ASAP: they'd hate to delay the procedure an hour
awaiting the okay from anesthesiology.

Three young women, interns, say hello between trips
to the toilet where you let the loss go, and go,

and go. But still no gyno appears to evaluate
the situation, mitigate the liquidation. Everyone passing

in scrubs, you both wonder, is it him? Him? No, too
scruffy. Too rough. Not nearly handsome enough.

While you are waiting and hurrying and losing,
you try your hand at fainting, twice: white-knuckle

the bathroom door, call out in slo-mo. Then just let go.
So nice to sink to the floor, stop looking for Dr. Right.

A sudden rush to converge: eight arms help you up. Take that,
triage — six hours later and I've got a cot of my own!

Then, he comes. Handsome, like you see on TV. You tease,
Got your attention, didn't I? He smiles: he's got a room booked

for your D & C. He will deal with your loss while you're under,
and for this, you thank him. When he's gone, you whisper,

Now *that's* a gynecologist! You and your husband laugh.
You do. But it's the laugh of survival.

*SUPPLEMENTARY

(*You Must Vote Yes or No*)

a.

You are the foreigner who speaks only
in metaphor: *I'm blasting the A/C
because the sun is a fried egg today.*

I am the teenager who speaks only
in simile: *so he's like, and then I'm like,
and it was just, so, like.*

be.

A shield
means you expect
to get hit.

A sword means
you plan
to take a swing.

see.

You want spaces in between
    not hard stops, just pauses
between our words. I know

you want to finish your own
   sentence, but love, we are parentheticals
that open and do not close.

de-

I hear what you're saying.
But not what you're meaning.

Swing, batter batter.

eee.

We are on opposite poles, having
claimed ours early. Your up is my
down, and oh, the vice versa.

Hope reversed. Are we
palindromic yet?
Don't nod.

TAR

i

Stone mammoths take a dip
in black ooze
frozen, here in
Miracle Mile

I learn the tar isn't hot
— not lava but asphalt
pushing its way
to the surface like oil

Methane bubbles
to bursting. Still, my mind
goes to boiling

Yours, to your funny
nephew, who calls the hot tub
hot sauce, the pool,
the cool

We wonder if we'll
have our own.

From this one block, millions
of specimens: insects, wolves
giant sloths, even bathing mammoths

(who didn't live with dinosaurs
— I'm only 65 million years off)

Back home, my appointment
is made: they'll draw
blood, count eggs

ii.

All specimens in the asphalt
are accidents. A bird gets its feet
stuck; predators descend, shocked
at their luck

Is it possible everything of any value
is an accident? We're optimistic,
want the universe
to take care of us

But we're out of our depth:
hear about the family
of saber tooth cats,
a mother and her four cubs

She'd wandered in for food,
her little ones coming in after

The anguish she must have felt
watching them starve
watching them

go under

We wonder if
nephews are enough

RING IN THE GRAIN

It's a strange party: these bodies, in a sort-of circle
around your mother's unhurried moans. She's gone,
vamoosed, not even in the room anymore. Had carried
you like twenty pounds of wet firewood.
Now, suddenly — your crown. Your wrapped hand.
The placenta, your cocoon, black in a bowl.

You're a boy: tuxedos, barbecues, the Superbowl.
One day you'll kiss a girl, then make good: slip that circle
of gold on her like your father's hand 'round your mother's hand.
Or maybe it will be a he, all limits on love gone
then. There are the men you could, should, would
and will be. So many possibilities to carry.

Absurd, our metaphors for the bundle your mom carries:
a newborn pup, a porcelain doll, a cashew nut, a bowling
ball. You lie there, incomprehensible, on the hardwood.
You're responsible for tides, brownouts, crop circles,
and just when I think I've got you figured out, you go
and change. Become more — human. You've got to hand

it to us. The book of man charts the roots of a hand,
the blunt hammer of foot, our veins like rivers carrying
us as close to the end of the world as we want to go.
Vestigial shoulder-wings; the back's shallow bowl.
Breasts, irises, every cell, our blood pumping: circular:
evidence of forethought. We are made of the same wood.

I know your kind...storied creatures of the woods.
Pink-cheeked, fuzzy-headed, round-eyed boys, hand
in hand in a ragged posy-holding sort-of circle.
By day, collecting berries and nuts, all your pockets can carry.
Twilight, gathering frogs in carved cedar bowls.
They squirm from your grasp and leap — and gone —

understanding comes and then, of course, goes.
That's what understanding does. Still, I'm sure I'd
know your face reflected, warped, in the shiny bowl
of a spoon. And your hands. On the spoon. Such small hands.
Now it's all instinct: the records our sleepy cells carry.
We're the history of man. In his square, in his circle.

Time to get going, baby. The future's circling.
The world's a wooden bowl I'll happily carry
to the party. Coming? Just give me your hand.

ROOTS:

THE SALLY DRAPER POEMS

SALLY DRAPER AT THE PREMIERE OF JAWS

I recognize that beach. Something about it — even in the dark.

Hey, Martha's Vineyard!
Shhhh!
Jeez.

I whisper to him. *We used to go there in summer.*
He rolls his eyes.

We're under the surface now, with the girl.
She has pretty legs, like a dancer.
They hired that girl just for her legs.

He looks at me. Pleading.
Sorry.
She treads water. I suck in my stomach.

The cold water's just making me colder.
They sure did crank the A/C— to the point
I barely remember that it's June.
They made it cold in here
so we'd cuddle up to our boys.

This is me flirting. I know I'm doomed.
He doesn't look at me. I guess to not
encourage more talking.

The sound kicks in, and I jump a little.
Da-da. Da-da. Da-da. I recognize it as a tuba
from the years Bobby practiced in the basement.
Stuck with that fat thing after being out sick
the day instruments were picked. I take it in. Know
the notes. *E-F. EF, EF, EF.*

I don't turn to him. Don't tell him about the tuba.
Now that I'm quiet, he takes my hand. Rubs
it between his to warm me up.

I know it's supposed to be scary
but they won't let this girl be hurt. They can't.

SALLY DRAPER'S FIRST KISS

I knew kissing a boy would be different when it wasn't your brother, I just couldn't imagine how. I'd turned my hand into a mouth, like Senor Wences (but didn't let him talk). Brought my hand close, really slowly, shut my eyes most of the way, keeping them open just a slit so I could see, too. Tasted the salt on my fingers; tried to imagine what the hole of my hand was tasting. I'd stuck my tongue in, but there was nothing there, just air.

When finally I made James stay still so I could kiss him, I knew what had been missing: resistance. I slipped my tongue through his teeth, happy he put up a fight. The kiss made me want to pee and made me want to kiss him again. Then James wanted to keep going, and I got distracted by the TV.

Now, whenever I see a ventriloquist — or puppets, Pinocchio, any wooden boy, boy on a string, boy with a hand inside him — I have to excuse myself.

SALLY DRAPER STRUGGLES TO BUY A CHRISTMAS GIFT

He's got no hobbies —
doesn't fish or golf
like other men.
He's not cultured.
Wouldn't care about
opera tickets,
or the new Neil
Diamond. A magazine
subscription's out,
of course. The ads.
He might wear a tie,
but I can't bear to buy
him something so dull.
So I choose *The Spy*
Who Came In From the Cold.
Maybe he'll see
the symbolism —
a man wanting
out. Hope. The girl.
And if not,
maybe he'll at least
wonder
why this book, what does it mean,
and he'll realize I'm
interesting.

SALLY DRAPER BUYS RED LIPSTICK

The woman at Marshall's
lines my lips first, with *Brick*,
as in House,
as in Shit-A.
I make an O.

Next comes the stick: *Dare You.*
I want to say, You win!
I'll buy you, but you'll just
languish in a drawer
with *Hellbent* and *Taboo.*

All my life I have
shied from these lips — his
lips. Bowed and smacking
of blow-up doll...
Ode to an O.

But today I'll wear red.
The red of a cherry
on a sword in a virgin
cocktail I'll have to sip
through a straw.

SALLY DRAPER: UPWARDLY MOBILE

I've seen what happens when you don't push for it. Follow your dreams.
You may start pretty, but you get old fast. You become a secondary
character in your own life. A wife.

It's the kind of war you can't let them know you're waging. And you can't
ever fall asleep — or onto a mattress — while on watch.

What they don't tell you is, you still have to pay your dues. And your dues
may mean bringing coffee to men, again and again. A wife on the clock.

At home, my mother had it made and brought to her by the help. Something
I think about when I pour.

SALLY DRAPER CONTEMPLATES THE INTERSTELLAR MISSION

Apparently the planets are aligned,
so they can shoot (launch? dispatch?)
the two pods into deep space — they'll
hop from orbit to orbit, hitching lifts,
their trajectories curving out, dots
connecting to form a conch-like shell.
I guess Voyager is, kind of, a conch.
We've spoken into it, hoping sound travels.
Everything about the mission is designed
with beauty in mind: the hope of it all. The sounds
on the record (whales, that kiss from a mother
to her baby, and my favourite, thunder).
The fact there are two, a pair, twins,
a couple mated for life like swans.

So how come when I think of those things
hurtling out, carrying Earth's seeds, all I can
think is that we are fucking the universe
like a man fucks a woman, and I want to fuck
the world like that too?

SALLY DRAPER TAKES CARLA OUT FOR LUNCH

It's taken me a year to find
her. There's no maid directory.
There should be a system; something.

I'd no idea we could live with women
and they could be taken from us and we
could not even know their full names.

She cooked me hot dogs. She taught me
fractions. Once, she spanked me. I
deserved it, and she took no pleasure in it.

I wanted to take her to a nice restaurant, but
on the phone she said no. The lunch counter
at Woolworth's it is.
                    When she arrives

she looks the same to me. Except my size,
instead of the powerful figure she'd been.
I stand to hug her, but she sits before I can.

She orders a clubhouse. I barely eat
my salad. I tell her about college. Classes,
living with the girls.

She tells me things have been fine,
she went to work for another family,
with twins. Smart boys. Nice boys.

I tell her she should have pulled the toothpick out
of her sandwich first. She smiles. Pulls
it out. It comes out clean, and I feel sick.

When I can't stop the tears from coming,
she holds out her napkin. Then changes
her mind, daubs at my eyes.

I thought. I thought.
She says, *I know, sweet pea.*
      You know, you're nothing like her.

She doesn't know what she's talking about.
When I get back home I dye my hair
a dull yet shocking shade of black.

SALLY DRAPER ON DOCTORS

As soon as she came out,
I bought Surgeon Barbie. Her scrubs
are short, it's true. Still, score
one for us. I put her box
on my desk for when I study.

I will worship no idols beyond thee!

*

Then it's Miss America Barbie.
For a laugh, I buy her too. Put
them side by side. But one day
I come home drunk and open her
so I can comb her hair.

I will worship no god but irony.

*

He asks me which I'd rather be:
the career girl or the beauty. Of course,
I say the surgeon. He knows it's true.
What I don't say? My doctor, dentist, gynecologist,
therapist…men. Always will be.

I worship you in hopes you'll worship me.

SALLY DRAPER HEARS THE NEWS

I get the call. Feel my face
go cold. The lion can't die.

No tears, yet — not 'til
I'm on the subway, really
trying not to cry. I let a man
give me his seat, and ride
in comfort all the way uptown.

At the wake, I speak, read
Yeats, though I know
he'd have preferred O'Hara.
Tougher. But tough,
the day isn't for him.
It's for us, the living.

And I wait for it. The fire.
I expect it to ignite in me,
his fire, it's my
right, I'm the eldest,
the heir. But the cold
persists. A cold there's no
coming in from.

Twice a week, I try
his death on for size.
A coat of imaginary grief
I'll wear like armour.

I should send a card
for his birthday this year.

SALLY DRAPER'S FIRST ABORTION

Junior year is hard on the girls. Two got married
and quit school. One became a drunk and flunked.
Then there's me, failing for no good reason
and for the first time, two men in one month.

They ask me who's picking me up —
I lie. Say my brother, though I haven't called either
in weeks. I'll take a cab home, have a nap.
Then study. Clean the kitchen. Be useful.

Except: I didn't know you were awake
when they did it. I guess I imagined being under.
A calculated fainting, then woken with smelling salts
by ladies in waiting — my problems gone. But no.

Bet she never wondered what kind of mother
she'd be...I call her. There's no answer. I will not cry.
They say a name, the name I gave them, the other
me, and I stand. Put on my father's face.

So this is what it's like to be brave.

SALLY DRAPER WILL NEVER DO MESCALINE AGAIN

It's natural. It's from a cactus. Native Americans
in *Mehico* have been using it
for thousands of years.

                 Yeah, but there weren't cars you could get hit by.
                   Or fifth-storey windows to jump out of.

Do you trust yourself, Sally?

                                 Not really.

                 Just, put it in a drink or something.
                         I don't want to taste it.

Even you have limits for what you'll
put in your mouth, huh?

                                 Funny.

Now we wait. Soon the backs of our
eyelids will be like stained glass.

Puff, the magic dragon, lived by the sea…

                     My dad used to sing me that song.
                     But he'd turn *Little Jackie Paper*
                         into *Little Sally Draper…*

That's sweet.

                                 Ehn.

That song's about grass. You want some?

It is not. And yes.

It's a well documented fact. Ask anyone.

[Without warning, it hits me. I want to ask him.
I want to call, wake him up, beg him
not for the truth
but for what I want to hear.
He was always good
at what I want to hear. But
I don't know his number
off by heart, I'd have to call
information.]

I'm feeling pretty good. How about you, Sall...?
Sallster? I'm sall...ivating. For you.

Shut up.

Are you crying?

I'm Jackie, and I'm Puff.
I left and am left behind.

I am going to be like this
for the rest of my life.

Would that be so bad?

[...]

95

NOTES

Liner Notes is for Madison. It was originally published in *PRISM International*, for which it received a Silver National Magazine Award.

The poems in *Papa Hotel* were originally published in a longer form. They are for my dad, Pete — a mystery, and a man.

Fever was written for Sachiko Murakami's Project Rebuild, projectrebuild.ca.

Cloud Sisters was written for Dawn Edmonds. My other cloud sisters are Catherine Bermingham and Marita Dachsel.

Tar is for my sweet nephews, Gabriel and Julian, and for Julie.

Ring in the Grain was written for Atticus. Maybe he will share it with Avner and Harriet.